A Colony of Bees

Heinemann Library
Chicago, Illinois

Richard and Louise Spilsbury

Customer Service 888-454-2279

Visit our website at www.heinemannlibrary.com

Originated by Dot Gradations Ltd
Printed in Hong Kong, China by Wing
  King Tong

08 07 06 05 04
10 9 8 7 6 5 4 3 2 1

Library of Congress Cataloging-in-Publication Data
Spilsbury, Louise.
  A colony of bees / Louise and Richard Spilsbury.
    p. cm. -- (Animal groups)
Includes bibliographical references and index.
  ISBN 1-4034-4688-1 (HC lib. bdg.) 1-4034-5414-0 (PB)
  1. Bees--Juvenile literature. I. Spilsbury, Richard, 1963-
II. Title.
III. Series.
  QL565.2.S65 2004
  595.79'9--dc21

                    2003010347

Acknowledgments
The author and publishers are grateful to the following
for permission to reproduce copyright material:

p. 4 NHPA/Mark Bowler; p. 5 Nature Picture Library/Jim
Clare; pp. 6, 10, 16 Oxford Scientific Films/Scott
Camazine; pp. 7, 19 NHPA/Stephen Dalton; p. 9 Nature
Picture Library/Dietmar Nill; p. 11 FLPA/Ray Bird; p. 12
FLPA/S. & D. & K. Maslowski; p. 13 Oxford Scientific
Films/Paulo De Oliveira; p. 14 Oxford Scientific
Films/Zebra Films Ltd/SAL; pp. 15, 20, 22 Oxford
Scientific Films; p. 17 FLPA/Minden Pictures/Konrad
Wothe; pp. 18, 21 Oxford Scientific Films/Satoshi
Kuribayashi; p. 24 Oxford Scientific Films/Lee
Lyon/SAL; p. 25 (top) Nature Picture Library/Lynn
Stone; p. 25 (bottom) Nature Picture Library/David
Shale; p. 26 Oxford Scientific Films/John Brown; p. 27
Nature Picture Library/Pete Oxford; p. 28 Corbis/Treat
Davidson/FLPA.

Cover photograph of a group of bees reproduced with
permission of NHPA/Stephen Dalton.

Every effort has been made to contact copyright holders
of any material reproduced in this book. Any omissions
will be rectified in subsequent printings if notice is
given to the publisher.

Contents

Some words are shown in bold, **like this.** You can find out what they mean by looking in the glossary.

What Are Bees?

Bees are a kind of **insect.** There are at least 25,000 **species,** or different kinds, of bees in the world. The largest is the leaf-cutter bee, which measures almost 4 centimeters—about as long as your thumb. The smallest is the stingless bee of Brazil, which is only about 2 to 5 millimeters long. Most bees have black and yellow stripes, but some have red or orange patches or stripes and others are metallic green, blue, or even red.

What is an insect?

Insects are small animals with a body in three sections: head, **thorax,** and **abdomen.** Most insects have six legs and a pair of wings as adults. A hard, shell–like skin called an exoskeleton protects their insides.

This is a buff-tailed bumblebee.
A bee's eye is really many small eyes connected together.
The **antennae** are used to smell.
The **mandibles** are used for holding or cutting things.

antennae

eye

mandibles

4

Where do bees live?

Bees live in countries all over the world. They live in many different kinds of **habitats**, from **tropical** forests to cool meadows, and from city gardens to quiet, leafy woodlands. The only places you will not find bees are the freezing **Poles** and the hottest deserts.

Which bees live in groups?

Most bee species live alone, except when it is time to **mate.** These are the solitary bees. Some kinds of bees are **social** insects that spend their whole lives in groups. Groups of bees are called colonies. In this book we look at some of these social bees and focus mainly on the best-known kinds—honeybees and bumblebees.

This is a large colony of wild honeybees.

What Is a Bee Colony?

Some colonies of bees are very large. Honeybee colonies can contain up to 80,000 bees, but bumblebees tend to form smaller groups. A colony of bees is like an enormous family where everyone helps and depends on each other. There are three main kinds of bees in most colonies—**workers**, **drones**, and a **queen**. Each of the different kinds of bees has a particular job to do.

What does the queen do?

Most colonies have only one queen. The queen has just one job in life—to lay eggs every day. Whatever the size of the colony, she produces all of the colony's young. The queen is the mother of all the other bees. This means that all the bees in a colony are closely related.

The queen (center) is the biggest, most important member of the colony. She can lay her own weight in eggs every day— that is about 1,500 eggs!

What are drones?

Drones are the **male** bees in a colony. A drone's job is to **mate** with a queen so that she can begin to lay eggs and produce young. A small number of drones develop at certain times of the year. In large honeybee colonies, a few hundred drones hatch in summer. Most drones do not live long. Once they have mated, they die.

Worker bees

Worker bees are **females** that cannot lay eggs. As their name suggests, worker bees do all the work in the colony! They feed, clean, and take care of the queen. They make, clean, repair, and guard the nest. They also look after the queen, the eggs, and the young bees that hatch out of the eggs.

Workers are the smallest bees in a colony. Drones are bigger and have large eyes.

worker

drone

Do worker bees share jobs?

A worker's job usually changes as it gets older. At first, young adult workers feed **larvae**. When they are older, they move on to building and repairing the nest. Finally, they collect food for the colony.

How many bees are in a colony?

In an average honeybee colony in summer there might be 1 **queen**, 250 **drones**, 20,000 **workers** collecting food, 40,000 workers looking after the nest and young, 7,000 eggs, 10,000 larvae, and 20,000 **pupae**!

What is the life cycle of a bee?

Honeybees begin life as eggs about the same size as a comma on this page. After four days they hatch into larvae that the workers feed. Almost a week later the larvae stop feeding and become pupae. During this stage they change into adults, and after two weeks they are fully grown. Very few larvae become queens and drones—most become workers.

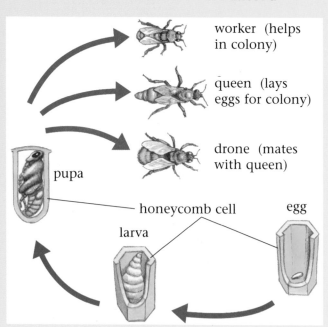

worker (helps in colony)

queen (lays eggs for colony)

drone (mates with queen)

pupa

honeycomb cell

larva

egg

How Does a Colony Start?

New bumblebee colonies begin each year when a new queen starts to lay eggs. In the fall, all workers, drones, and the old queen from an old bumblebee colony die. Only the new queen lives on.

In the spring, a new bumblebee queen finds a safe place to nest. She makes a **wax** pot, about the shape of a thimble, and lays about six eggs in it. The queen feeds and protects the larvae that hatch out of these eggs. When this first set of bees is fully grown, they take over the work. Then the queen returns to laying eggs. The workers enlarge the nest and feed and care for the queen and new larvae that hatch. This happens again and again so the colony gets bigger and bigger.

These worker bumblebees are busy building a new nest.

When do honeybee colonies start?

Honeybee colonies can last for many years. New colonies of honeybees usually form when an old colony becomes too crowded. The old **queen** leaves with some of the **workers** and **drones** to start another colony. These groups of flying bees are called **swarms** and they usually form in hot weather.

Back in the old colony, new queens are born. They fly out of the nest with some drones and **mate** in the air. One new queen will return to the original nest to lay eggs and take over the colony. The other queens go off to create new colonies elsewhere. If more than one queen returns to the original nest, the queen bees may fight until one becomes the new queen of the colony.

Honeybee swarms move together like a black cloud in the sky. When they land, they often form shapes like the one shown here.

Soon after new honeybee queens become adults, they fly out of the nest. Drones flying out of the nest mate with the queens in the air. This is called a nuptial, or wedding, flight.

What Is a Bee Nest?

Bees' nests come in many shapes and sizes. Some nests are the size of the palm of your hand, but others can be as long as a small car!

Honeybees may make their nests tucked away inside trees or buildings, although they sometimes make them hanging from branches in the open. Bumblebees usually make nests in holes in the ground—for example, in empty mouse **burrows**. A bee's nest is made up of many **cells,** which are like tiny rooms made out of **wax.** Bumblebee colonies build their wax cells inside balls of grass or moss. Their rounded, pot-shaped cells vary in size and shape. The cells in all bees' nests are used for young bees to grow in and to store food such as **honey.**

Bees usually make their nests in sheltered places, such as in old tree trunks.

Staying safe

A bee's nest usually has one entrance hole with a platform outside for bees to land on. **Workers** guard this so pests like wax-eating caterpillars cannot get in. Nests also have a waterproof layer to keep the rain out. This outer layer sometimes is made of **resin**. It helps hide the nest, too. One kind of bumblebee called the carder bee weaves bits of moss together to hide its nest.

How do bees take care of the nest?

Worker bees clean nests by removing waste, dirt, and spilled food. After spending all winter in the nest, honeybees have a big spring cleaning. Workers also fix any holes in the nest to keep out rain and cold air. They fill gaps with propolis, or bee's glue, which they collect from sticky buds of certain trees.

When carder bees cover their underground nest with moss they leave a single hole, through which they fly in and out.

What is a honeycomb?

A honeybee colony's nest is made of thousands of hexagonal, or six-sided, **cells** that fit together neatly. These are arranged in upright sections. Each section is called a **honeycomb.** Sometimes honeycombs are protected by a nest wall. Bees move through passageways between the wall and the honeycomb.

Inside a honeycomb

Inside the nest, **workers** use some of the honeycomb cells for storing food. These cells are usually nearest the top. Below these are cells for the worker eggs and **larvae.** The **queen** lays one egg in each cell. Workers make larger cells on the edge of honeycombs for new queens and **drones** to develop in. The cells in a honeycomb always slope downward from the top to the base. This stops things inside the cells from falling out.

This wild honeybee's nest is made up of seven honeycombs.

14

How Are Honeycombs Made?

Bee colonies make the **wax** they use to build their nests. The first ingredients are pieces of fat made in their **abdomen.** They chew these pieces, mixing them with the saliva, or spit, in their mouth. Different bees may mix other things in, too, such as soil, **resin**, or **pollen.**

Teamwork

A colony of bees can build honeycombs only because they work together. Teams of worker bees start with a ring of wax at the top of the nest and build downward. They do not build complete cells one by one. They make the sides of several cells next to each other at the same time.

How many cells do bees make?

Bee colonies usually make about six honeycombs inside a nest with a total of about 100,000 cells in them. It takes more than 4 pounds (2 kilograms) of beeswax to make a set of honeycombs like this!

Bees use their **mandibles** and legs to shape the soft wax into the cells of their honeycomb.

Keeping the right temperature

Bees need to be at a steady temperature of 95 °F (35 °C) to make the fatty pieces they need for **wax**. This is also the temperature that **larvae** need to grow properly. If the nest gets too hot, teams of honeybee workers beat their wings at the nest entrance to blow in cool air. If the nest gets too cold, bees warm up by eating **honey** for **energy** and shaking their wings. They also huddle together for warmth.

These bees are beating their wings at the entrance of their nest to cool it down.

How do they do that?

Honeybee workers measure each cell so that every one is exactly the right size. They test the size of each cell and the thickness of the cell walls using their **antennae**. Each cell wall of a honeycomb is usually 0.073 millimeters thick. If the wax is too thick in one spot, they scrape some off and use it somewhere else!

What Do Bees Eat?

Bees get all the food they need from the flowers of many different kinds of plants. They take **pollen** and **nectar** from the center of flowers. Pollen is high in **protein**, which animals need to build or repair body parts. Nectar gives bees the sugar they need for **energy**.

How do bees find food?

The bees from a particular colony usually feed from just two types of flower. Bees may travel up to one mile (two kilometers) from the nest to find the right ones. Bees find flowers by looking for their brightly colored petals and smelling the sweet scents of the flowers.

Bees fly well and they can move quickly between many flowers. The hairs on a bumblebee's **thorax** help keep its wing muscles warm so that it can fly in cool weather.

17

Collecting food

Bees suck up **nectar** using their proboscis, a drinking straw-shaped tongue that curls up when not in use. Bees store the nectar in a special pouch called a honey stomach. **Pollen** from the flower sticks to a bee's hairy coat. The bee's legs brush this pollen into a ball and into its pollen baskets to carry it home. Pollen baskets are hairless patches on a bee's back legs, surrounded by long hairs that form a basket shape.

Bees and flowers are a good example of the way plants and animals need each other to live.

What is pollination?

When bees visit flowers for food they also help to **pollinate** the flowering plants. When a bee crawls into a flower for nectar, some of the pollen attached to its body from a previous flower rubs off on the new one. The pollen fertilizes the second flower, which makes the flower produce seeds that can grow into new plants.

Do bees share food?

The **worker** bees that collect food for the colony return to the nest to share it with the bees working in the nest. They bring up the nectar from their honey stomach and pass it on by mouth. The bees in the nest eat some of this nectar and use some to make **honey**. Honeybees store honey for winter when the flowers of most plants have died and there is less food available.

When a wax cell is full of honey, honeybees seal it with wax to keep it fresh, just as we seal things in a jar with a lid.

How do bees make honey?

To make honey, bees mix nectar with saliva in their mouths and put droplets of the mixture into a **wax cell**. They leave it there and fan it with their wings to let some of the water from the nectar **evaporate** into the air. The sticky substance that is left is the honey.

19

What do larvae eat?

Adult bees eat some of the **pollen** they collect, but they feed most of it to the colony's **larvae. Protein** foods are often called bodybuilders, and bee larvae need protein-rich pollen to grow. When **workers** return to the nest with full pollen baskets, they store the pollen in **cells.** Other workers mix the pollen with **nectar** to form a mixture called beebread, which they feed to the larvae.

Worker bees feed larvae that are developing inside their wax cells.

What is royal jelly?

Royal jelly—or bee milk—is creamy-white and very rich in **vitamins** and protein. Worker bees make it by chewing pollen. They feed it to all larvae for the first two to three days of life. Larvae that will become workers or **drones** are then fed beebread, but those that will become **queen** bees continue to be fed royal jelly. This is because a queen needs lots of protein to be able to lay lots of eggs!

Do Bees Talk to Each Other?

Animals that live in groups need to be able to **communicate.** They need to pass information to each other about many different things, such as what is going on in the group and where to find food. Bee colonies communicate mostly by smell and taste, but they also tell each other things by doing special dances!

Do bees use scent to communicate?

Bees in a colony recognize each other and their enemies by scents called **pheromones.** The queen makes the most important pheromones. When workers lick and clean her, they pick up some of her scent and pass it on to the other bees. The smell and taste of it passes on information, such as what the queen needs. It also makes the whole colony share the same smell. This means that bees only need to smell another bee to know if it belongs to their colony.

When bees in a colony touch mouths to pass on food, they share the colony smell.

When it is time to **swarm**, honeybee queens give off a particular **pheromone** that attracts other bees to follow them to a new home. **Worker** bees also give off a particular pheromone to warn others of danger and call other workers to help them defend the colony.

For **tropical** stingless bees like these, workers leave trails of scent that lead other workers from the colony to the food. Worker bees know they are getting closer to the food when the scent gets stronger.

Why do bees buzz?

You have probably heard bees buzzing, which may sound as if they are communicating. In fact, buzzing is the sound made by the rapid beating of their wings. When a nest is disturbed, bees buzz louder because they are beating their wings faster to fan alarm scents through the colony. Honeybees can beat their wings over 11,000 times a minute!

Why do bees dance?

Worker bees from a honeybee colony are always on the lookout for new sources of food. When a worker bee finds one, it returns to the nest and performs a dance—a sequence of movements—on the side of the **honeycomb** to tell the others where the food source is.

Bees may dance in a circle shape, or in a shape like a number 8. The line the bee walks between the loops of the 8 tells the other bees how far to the left or right of the Sun they must go. The dancing bee wiggles its **abdomen** to show how far away the flowers are. The faster the wiggling, the closer the flowers are to the nest!

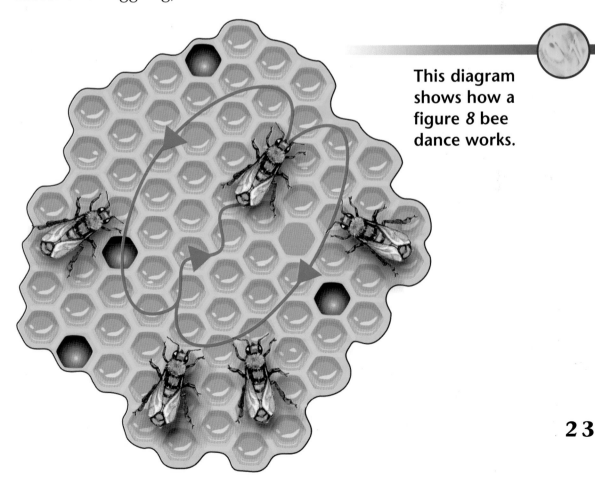

This diagram shows how a figure 8 bee dance works.

23

What Dangers Does a Bee Colony Face?

Some animals attack a bee colony to try to eat the **honey**, **larvae**, and sometimes the **wax**, inside. Bee **predators** include bears such as the sloth bear, skunks, and a kind of bird called a bee-eater. Tiny **insects** called varroa mites bite bees and give them a disease that has destroyed many wild honeybee colonies. People also harm bees when they spray **pesticides** and cut down trees and other places where they make nests.

The smartest predator?

The honeyguide bird must get the prize for smartest bee predator. Its beak cannot break open a nest, so it leads ratels—also called honey badgers—to bees' nests. Once the nest is found and broken, the bird and the ratel eat all they want.

The ratel gives off a scent that calms down the bees while it uses its tough claws to open their nest.

People who keep bees for their honey keep them in artificial nests called hives. Beekeepers have to wear protective clothing because when a bee colony is disturbed, worker bees may fly out and attack.

In some countries, such as Nepal, honey hunters take honey from wild nests. They usually leave enough honey for the bee colony to survive.

How does a colony defend itself?

Most **queen** and **worker** bees have stingers they use to attack enemies. A bee's stinger is formed from a tube at the end of its **abdomen**. A stinger pierces the skin of an animal and injects poison into it. If a honeybee stings a large animal, barbs on the stinger hook into the skin and pull the bee's stinger out, killing the bee. This does not happen when the stinger is used on another insect.

What are killer bees?

Africanized honeybees are also called killer bees. These bees behave normally when hunting for food, but if they sense their colony is in danger, they defend it angrily. If large numbers attack animals or people nearby, they can kill because they deliver so many stings at once.

This is a killer bee. Angry killer bees may pursue animals for long distances to defend their colony.

How Does a Colony Change?

Bumblebee colonies that live in places with cold winters change a lot each year. Almost all the bumblebees in the colony die because they do not store enough **honey** to survive winter when few flowers bloom. Only some young **queens** survive. They hibernate by going into a deep sleep underground or in a pile of leaves. Then they wake up again in the spring to start a new colony.

Do honeybee colonies change?

Honeybee colonies change less than bumblebee colonies. **Workers** only live for about six weeks in summer, the busiest time of year. Those born in late fall stay with the colony all winter. Any **drones** still around are not allowed back into the nest, so they die.

In the fall, remaining honeybee workers and their queen huddle together in the nest and eat stored honey to survive the cold winter months.

27

What happens if a queen dies?

Honeybee colonies change in the summer when **swarms** leave to form new colonies. They also change when a **queen** dies. A queen honeybee can live for about five years, but as she grows older, she produces less **pheromone**. This acts as a message to tell **workers** to start feeding **royal jelly** to future queens and to prepare **drones** to **mate** with them. However, if a new queen tries to take over before the old queen is ready, the old queen kills her with her stinger!

Do new queens ever lead swarms?

In stingless bees, old queens become too fat to fly when the colony gets overcrowded. Young queens lead swarms away to form new colonies, taking **honey**, **pollen**, and **wax** with them. The old queen stays behind in the old colony.

Bees in a colony know all about their queen from her scent. News about the queen can spread to every bee in a colony within fifteen minutes!

Bee Facts

What does "busy as a bee" mean?

You probably have heard the phrase "busy as a bee," but have you thought about what it means? It refers to someone who is always doing something useful, like the worker bees in a colony.

How far can bees fly?

Honeybees can fly up to 8 miles (14 kilometers) away from their nest when they go looking for food. Most of the time they only go 1 mile (up to 2 kilometers) in a single trip. Bees usually fly at about 9 miles (15 kilometers) an hour, but their top speed may be around 18 miles (30 kilometers) an hour!

Do bees help people?

Bees and bee products are incredibly useful to people. Bees **pollinate** most of the food plants in the world. Honey is a healthy food that sometimes is used to fight certain infections. Some people even eat royal jelly because they think it improves health.

Does all honey taste the same?

Honey can taste very different! The taste and color of honey depends on the flowers the bees in a colony take their **nectar** from. For example, honey made from clover flowers looks and tastes different from honey made from fruit tree blossoms.

How much honey can bees make?

Honeybees have to collect nectar from more than five million flowers to make just 2 pounds (1 kilogram) of honey! In just one year a colony may collect more than 220 pounds (100 kilograms) of nectar! With this they make more than 40 pounds (18 kilograms) of honey to survive the winter.

Glossary

abdomen   third or lower section of an insect's body

antenna (more than one are called **antennae**) feeler on an insect's head that comes in a pair

burrow below-ground dwelling

cell   tiny box that holds young or stores honey and pollen in a honeycomb

communicate   pass on information

drone   male bee

energy   what animals produce from food in order to live and grow

evaporate   turn from a liquid into a gas

female   animal that, when grown up, can become a mother

habitat   where an animal or group of animals live

honey   sweet syrup bees make for their food

honeycomb   group of hexagonal (six-sided) cells built of beeswax

insect   small, six-legged animal that, as an adult, has a body divided into three sections

larva (more than one are called **larvae**) young, not fully formed insect

male   animal that, when grown up, can become a father

mandible   jaw

mate/mating   produce young. When bees mate, a drone puts sperm inside a queen bee's body to fertilize the eggs inside her.

nectar   sweet, sugary juice flowers make to attract bees

pesticide   spray some farmers use to kill insects that feed on plants

pheromone   perfume-like substance

Poles   northernmost and southernmost points on Earth

pollen   powder flowers make that makes seeds grow when it lands in another flower

pollinate   when pollen moves from one flower to another

predator   animal that hunts or catches other animals to eat

protein   substance in food that helps animals grow strong

pupa (more than one are called **pupae**) stage in growth just before an insect becomes an adult

queen   bee that lays all the eggs in a colony

resin   sticky substance some plants and trees make

royal jelly   milky food worker bees make

social   live in a group

species   group of living things that are similar and can produce healthy offspring together

swarm   large group of insects that move while staying very close together

thorax   middle part of an insect's body

tropical   area with some of the hottest temperatures in the world

vitamins   nutrients that keep an animal healthy

wax   substance bees use to make honeycombs

worker   female bee that does all the work in a bee colony

More Books to Read

Glaser, Linda. *Brilliant Bees*. Brookfield, Conn.: Millbrook Press, 2003.

Loewen, Nancy. *Busy Buzzers: Bees in Your Backyard*. Minneapolis: Picture Window Books, 2003.

McDonald, Mary Ann. *Bees*. Eden Prairie, Minn.: The Child's World, Inc., 2003.

Nelson, Robin. *From Flowers to Honey*. Minneapolis: Lerner Publishing Group, 2002.

Penny, Malcolm. *Bees*. Chicago: Raintree, 2003.

Riley, Joelle. *Buzzing Bumblebees*. Minneapolis: Lerner Publishing Group, 2003.

Tagliaferro, Linda. *Bees and Their Hives*. Minnetonka, Minn.: Capstone Press, 2004.

Index